Prayers and Affirmations
for a Life of Faith, Happiness
and Awe in God

JEFF DOLES

Personal Confessions from the Psalms

© 2012 by Jeff Doles. All rights reserved.

Published by
Walking Barefoot Ministries
P.O. Box 1062, Seffner, FL 33583

ISBN: 978-0-9823536-1-5

All scripture quotations, unless otherwise indicated, are taken from the New King James Version. © 1982 by Thomas Nelson, Inc. Used by permission. All rights reserved.

Scripture quotations marked NASB are taken from the New American Standard Bible®, © The Lockman Foundation 1960, 1962, 1963, 1968, 1971, 1972, 1973, 1975, 1977, 1995. Used by permission. All rights reserved.

Cover photo © iStockphoto 9339689
Cover design and book interior by
www.ChristianBookDesign.com

For more resources on enjoying new life in Christ, living in faith and the power of the Holy Spirit, or to find out more about Jeff Doles, visit our websites:

www.WalkingBarefoot.com
www.TheFaithLog.com
www.JeffDoles.com

CONFESSIONS

Introduction: Confessing the Psalms 7

Psalm 1 ~ The Happiness   17
Psalms 3-4 ~ A Shield All Around Me   18
Psalm 5 ~ My King   19
Psalm 16 ~ The Portion of My Inheritance   19
Psalm 18 ~ My Strength in Time of Struggle   21
Psalm 19 ~ The Instruction of Yahweh   22
Psalm 20 ~ My Help From Heaven   23
Psalm 21 ~ Victorious Joy   24
Psalm 23 ~ My Shepherd   25
Psalm 25 ~ My Whole Life   26
Psalm 26 ~ Yahweh Clears My Name   27
Psalm 27 ~ The Goodness of Yahweh in My Life   28
Psalm 28 ~ Yahweh's Treasured Ones   29
Psalm 32 ~ The Happiness of Being Forgiven   30
Psalm 34 ~ A Brag About Yahweh   31
Psalm 35 ~ Yahweh Contends for Me   33
Psalm 36 ~ The Covenant Love of Yahweh   34
Psalm 37 ~ Possess the Land in Patience   34
Psalm 40 ~ Yahweh, My Rescue   36
Psalm 41 ~ The Happiness of Being Helped   38
Psalm 46 ~ Abundantly Available Help   38
Psalm 52 ~ Like a Green Olive Tree   40
Psalm 56 ~ Yahweh is For Me   40
Psalm 57 ~ Yahweh in the Storm   41
Psalm 61 ~ When My Heart is Overwhelmed   42

Psalm 62 ~ God My Calm   43

Psalm 63 ~ Yahweh is Life and Joy   44

Psalm 66 ~ What Yahweh Has Done for Me   45

Psalm 71 ~ Yahweh All My Days   47

Psalm 73 ~ A Sudden Realization   48

Psalm 77 ~ The Tenacity of Faith   50

Psalm 81 ~ Fully Satisfied in Yahweh   52

Psalm 84 ~ Yahweh's Dwelling Place   53

Psalm 85 ~ The Glory of Yahweh in Our Land   54

Psalm 91 ~ My Sheltering Place   55

Psalm 92 ~ The Hand of Yahweh in My Life   57

Psalm 94 ~ Yahweh Sets Things Right   58

Psalm 101 ~ Honoring Yahweh   59

Psalm 103 ~ Yahweh's Benefits   60

Psalm 112 ~ A Life Well-Lived   62

Psalm 115 ~ All My Glory is in Yahweh   63

Psalm 116 ~ Why I Love Yahweh   64

Psalm 118 ~ Giving Thanks to Yahweh   66

Psalm 121 ~ I Turn to Yahweh   69

Psalm 126 ~ Yahweh Frees the Captives   70

Psalm 127 ~ A Legacy in Yahweh   71

Psalm 128 ~ The Extravagant Blessing   72

Psalm 130 ~ Forgiveness and Help   73

Psalm 131 ~ Quieting Myself in Yahweh   74

Psalm 133 ~ Where the Anointing Flows   75

Psalm 136 ~ Yahweh's Faithful Love for Me   76

Psalm 138 ~ Before All the Kings of the Earth   77

Psalm 139 ~ Yahweh Knows Me   78

Psalm 140 ~ His Victory Over My Enemies   81

Psalm 141 ~ Help in a Time of Evil   82

Psalm 142 ~ When I Feel Abandoned   83

Psalm 143 ~ When My Soul Feels Weak   84

Psalm 144 ~ From Battle to Blessing   86

Psalm 145 ~ My King and My God   87

Psalm 146 ~ All My Life is All About Him   90

End Notes   93

Introduction: Confessing the Psalms

Every month for about the past 25 years I have followed the practice of praying through the book of Psalms. The math works out quite handily: 150 psalms divided by 30 days in a month comes to 5 psalms a day. So each day I pray through five psalms, beginning with the first five on the first day of the month, the second five on the second day, and so on. Now, that does not mean that I necessarily make it through all five each day. Some days I am caught by one psalm in particular. Some days by just a section of a psalm. Some days by just a single verse, and I spend my prayer time on that.

The constancy of this habit has been very rewarding for me. I have discovered that the more I pray the psalms, the more sensitive I become to them and the more they open up inside me, sometimes like an overstuffed suitcase springing wide open when I pop the latch. I never know, from day to day, which portion might hold a fresh revelation for me.

Creating confessions such as the ones in this book is one way I have learned to meditate on the psalms, repeating them over and over to myself, personalizing them, instructing my soul with them. David, God's premier psalm writer, must have known something about this process because he learned how to encourage himself in the LORD during difficult times. When he and his band of soldiers returned home to Ziklag, they discovered that it had been burned with fire, and their wives and children were carried off by the Amalekites. The Bible says they wept bitter tears until they simply had no more power to weep. For David, it was even worse, because he was their leader, and his men were so consumed by grief that there was talk of stoning him. David was in distress, and it might have destroyed him completely, except for this: "David strengthened himself in the LORD his God" (1 Samuel 30:1-6).

We are not told what that looked or sounded like, but I imagine it included singing some of the psalms he had written, going over again the many times he had experienced the faithfulness of God in his life, confessing them over and over to his soul until he was ready to rise up, pursue and "recover all" (1 Samuel 30:8). However, I do know that confessing the psalms has often helped *me* encourage *myself* in the LORD.

What is a Confession?

Someone once asked me if our ministry taught "positive confession." I answered that we teach about speaking in agreement with the Word of God ~ and that is what I mean by "confession." For many, the word "confess" has only a negative connotation: to admit to wrongdoing, or to acknowledge some inconvenient truth. However, it also has a very positive use, such as when it is used to speak of confessing the faith.

The basic meaning of "confess" is to acknowledge or give assent. In the New Testament, the Greek word translated "confess" is *homologeo,* from *homou,* "same," and *lego,* to "say." To confess is to "say the same thing," to speak in agreement with what is being said about something. For example, when we confess our sins, as in 1 John 1:9, we are agreeing with God that we have done things we ought not to have done, and that we need to be forgiven and cleansed because of them. When we confess the Lord Jesus, as in Romans 10:9, we are agreeing and affirming that Jesus is indeed our God and King.

Years ago, during a very difficult time in my life, I began making confessions like the ones in this book, learning to speak in agreement with the Word of God. I knew it would take a strong, bold faith if I was going to get the turnaround I desperately needed. So I gathered together a number of Scripture promises, cast them in the first person and began speaking them out. Just reading them silently to myself would not be enough ~ I knew I had to get them down deep into my heart. With the heart we believe, with the mouth we confess (Romans 10:10), and "out of the abundance of the heart the mouth speaks" (Matthew 12:24). So I started reading them out loud. Though it was awkward at first, I kept at it, day after day, pacing up and down the hallway of my home, reading and repeating these promises. The more I did this, the bolder I got, speaking them out louder and louder until I got to where I was shouting them out with great passion.

What was I doing? I was letting them fill my eyes, my mind, my mouth and my ears ~ and before long, they began to fill my heart in abundance. It was a sort of defibrillation, you might say, shocking my heart back into the rhythms of faith with the Word of God. I was recalibrating my thoughts and emotions with the promises of God and realigning my will with the heart of God. And after about a month, I began to see breakthrough. Ever since then, my life has been different and I have walked in a deeper level of faith and joy.

The Name of the Lord

In these confessions, I frequently refer to God by the name *Yahweh*. This a commonly accepted pronunciation of the four

Hebrew letters that comprise the personal name of God in the Old Testament. Transliterated into English, they are YHWH (or YHVH). In most English translations, this name is indicated by the word "Lord" (all capital letters). We also find it in shortened form, for example, in the word "Hallelujah" which means "Praise *Yah*."

I prefer to use "Yahweh" instead of "Lord," because it is the name by which God has revealed Himself in covenant with His people. *God* and *Lord* and *King* speak of what He is. They are titles of His office, and I love them all. However, He invites us into personal relationship with Himself, so I like using the personal name He has revealed, especially since I am confessing these Psalms in terms of that relationship. Should it turn out, as some think, that this is not the correct way to pronounce His name, I figure it is no more incorrect than to pronounce it as *Lord*.

As a Christian, I understand "Yahweh" or "the Lord" in the Old Testament to be the God who has always existed in three persons ~ Father, Son and Holy Spirit. The name Jesus, in Hebrew, is *Yeshua*, and means "Yahweh Saves." The Hebrew word often used for "salvation" in the psalms is *yeshuah*, which speaks of the salvation that comes from the Lord. So, whenever I come across it, I think of Jesus because I know it is ultimately talking about Him (indeed, *all* the Scriptures are ultimately about Him) and I always remember that there are many aspects to the salvation God has for us in Him. The range of meaning includes deliverance, healing, victory, preservation and prosperity. The specific meaning in any given passage is determined by the context. But since the salvation we have in Jesus includes all of those things, the meaning I have in mind when I speak these confessions is the one that is most appropriate to my life at the time.

About the Psalms

Praying the psalms for twenty-five years, I have learned that there are many moods and styles. Some are wisdom psalms, some celebrate the reign of the king, some are offerings of praise and thanksgiving, some are laments, and some are imprecatory (where the writer prays for God to bring judgment upon the enemy). Sometimes the psalm writer is disappointed, disoriented, even depressed. However, every one of them is called *tehillah*, a psalm, a praise to God, because in each one the psalm writer brings his thanks, his joy, his sorrow, his disappointment, his anger ~ whatever is going on in his heart ~ to Yahweh.

Although there are 150 psalms, there are only 60 confessions in this book. I do not attempt to offer a translation of the psalms, or a treatment of *all* the psalms, or even a complete treatment of *any* of the psalms I have selected here. They are not in any way intended to replace traditional uses of the psalms. Quite the opposite, my desire is that these would encourage you not only to read the psalms but to assist you in praying them yourself. I offer these confessions simply as prayers and affirmations adapted from the psalms.

In some instances, I make a personal confession where the psalm writer makes a petition. I do this because I understand and confess the psalms through the New Testament reality of Jesus the Messiah and what the coming of His kingdom into the world means for us. In Him is the fulfillment of all the promises and prophecies God made to His people. So, for example, where the psalm writer says, "Contend with those, Yahweh, who contend with me" (Psalm 35:1, my version), I am mindful that Jesus has already done that for me: He took on the devil and death and sin ~ everything that stood against us ~ nailed it to the cross and rose victoriously from the dead three days later. "Who shall separate us from the love of Christ? Shall tribulation, or distress, or persecution, or famine, or nakedness, or peril, or sword? …

Yet in all these things we are more than conquerors through Him who loved us" (Romans 8:35-37). I do not petition God to do that for me ~ it has already been accomplished! What I do, then, is confess the reality of it.

The book of Psalms belongs as much to the Church as to ancient Israel, since the apostle Paul describes all believers in Jesus, whether from among the Gentiles or the Jews, as being *grafted on* to the root stock of Israel (Romans 11:17-24). The good news of the gospel is that, in Jesus the Messiah, we are heir to all the promises of God. Indeed, Jesus is the mediator of a new and better covenant, one that is based on even better promises than the old one, and cut in His own blood (Hebrews 8:6; Luke 22:20).

There is a strong community dimension to the book of Psalms. It was not just Israel's prayer book but also its hymnal. The psalms were meant to be sung together by the people as a congregation. King David even established choirs for singing them, and many of the psalms come from these choirs (e.g., psalms by Asaph, Heman, and the sons of Korah). Singing or praying the psalms together has also been a part of the Church from the beginning. For the Church as well as for ancient Israel, psalms express the heart of the community of faith in covenant relationship with God.

Of course, there is also a strong personal dimension to the psalms. David did not pray, "The LORD is *our* Shepherd," but "The LORD is *my* Shepherd." However, that confession belongs to the community of faith and everyone in it, to claim and confess together and individually. So, though we may pray the psalms in private, we never pray them privately. They never belong just to us, even as we do not belong just to ourselves but to each other in the community of faith. Psalms express the heart of the individual in covenant relationship with Yahweh and with the rest of the community. Most importantly, they express the heart of God in relationship with all His people.

Who is the Enemy?

As I noted above, some psalms are imprecatory in nature, where the psalm writer calls on God to contend with the enemy, to rain down judgment and bring the adversary to justice. Many of the confessions in this book do deal with that. Not by petition, however, but by affirming the work God has already done through Jesus. Please understand, though, that people are *not* the enemy. Though there may are nations or leaders or groups who come against the people of God, in large ways or small, they are not the real adversary.

The real adversary is the demonic influence that is behind them, motivating and influencing them. The apostle Paul refers to these as "principalities and powers." But the good news of the gospel is that Jesus the Messiah has "disarmed the principalities and powers" and "made a public spectacle of them, triumphing over them in it" (Colossians 2:15). He did this by the cross and the resurrection. God has also seated Him as King, "far above all principality and power and might and dominion" (Ephesians 1:21). They must all acknowledge that Jesus is Lord, that all authority has been given to Him in heaven and on earth (Philippians 2:9-11; Matthew 28:18).

Exuberant Joy

The psalms are full of great celebration and rejoicing. There are many Hebrew words used to express this, words that give us vivid pictures and describe great exuberance, but they have often been flattened out in our English translations. In the psalms, joy is not a quiet "knowing in the heart," it actually looks and sounds like something. You can shout for joy, sing for joy, cry out for joy, "creak" for joy, jump for joy, spin for joy. Joy is lighthearted, at times even giddy. So, in my confessions you will find me dancing and jumping and whirling and hooting and howling and hollering, even letting out a *Yahoo!* Don't be afraid, then, to let the joy of Jesus overtake you and come out in whatever way it wants.

Let the Lines Work on You

Shortly after I first began learning to pray the psalms, I had the opportunity of going on a couple of retreats with a group of Presbyterian men to the Monastery of the Holy Spirit, a community of Cistercian monks in Conyers, GA. On both occasions, Father Gus (Dom Augustine Moore) spoke with us about prayer, particularly about praying the psalms. He had entered the order as a young man, at Gethsemani Abbey, in Trappist, KY, and was now quite advanced in years. He had come to a lot of wisdom in those years and at one time served as the abbot at Holy Spirit Monastery. Since I was just beginning to learn the psalms in those days, I was very much interested in what he would have to say.

Two things stand out for me from those talks. First, he said that, as he prayed the psalms: "I let the lines work on me." The steady rhythm of praying the lines of the psalms, day after day, year after year, formed him, and transformed him. Second, he said that as he prayed, he would sometimes feel that he was being "zoomed by the Holy Spirit." At the time, I did not know what he might have meant by that, but I believe I have since come to understand and experience it for myself.

I have carried these two things from Father Gus' talks with me as I have continued to pray through the psalms. The lines have indeed worked on me and changed my life. They have become a conversation, a relationship, between me and God. Simply put, in the psalms, I speak to God and God speaks to me. This has set some things in me that have become very precious ~ I have come to see God's great desire, not just for me but for all people, for the nations and the generations. I find myself interceding for them often, simply in praying through the psalms.

Praying the psalms has been defibrillating for my heart. Line by line, it has been bringing my heart into alignment with the heart of God. I have also often experienced what I would call the "zoom" of the Holy Spirit while praying the psalms ~ times of deep joy, or intense peace, or unexpected compassion for others, or even the inarticulate groaning of the Spirit that Paul talks about in Romans 8:26.

Sustaining the Weary One with a Word

For many years now, my favorite verse, the one I come back to again and again, is not from the psalms but from the prophets: "The Lord GOD has given me the tongue of disciples, that I may know how to sustain the weary one with a word. He awakens me morning by morning, He awakens my ear to listen as a disciple" (Isaiah 50:4 *NASB*). That has been my desire with this project, indeed, with all my writing and ministry ~ to sustain the weary one with a word.

As I have worked on these psalm confessions, developing them, reading them, speaking them out loud, I have felt the peace of God and the joy of Jesus rising up inside me, and faith rising up along with it. I believe these are words that will sustain the weary one, because they are based on the Word that comes from God. But don't just read them. Find a place where you can say them out loud, maybe even where you can shout them out with passion. Let them go up with a whoop and a holler to God, with the velocity of faith, and watch what happens in your heart and in your life.

Psalm 1 ~ The Happiness

O the happiness!
I do not walk in the counsel
Of those who are ungodly;
I do not seek out
Or follow their advice.
I do not stand in the path
With those who purpose
To do what is wrong.
I do not sit with those
Who mock what is good.

But my delight
Is in the instruction of Yahweh,
I think about it all the time.

So I am like a tree
Planted by rivers of water,
Established,
Well-rooted,
Well-fed,
That bears its fruit abundantly
In its season,
And its leaf does not wither.
Whatever I do prospers.

The judgment of Yahweh is for me,
Not against me.
I stand with the people
Who stand in awe of Him,
And Yahweh watches over my path.
O the happiness.

Psalms 3-4 ~ A Shield All Around Me

Yahweh is a shield all around me.
He is the One in whom I glory,
The One who lifts up my head.
I cry out to Him
And He hears me.

I lie down and sleep;
I awake, for He sustains me.
I will not fear,
Even if 10,000 foes come against me
And surround me on every side.
For Yahweh will rise up to deliver me.

My help, my rescue,
My victory, my prosperity,
My salvation comes from Yahweh.
His blessing is upon His people.

There are many who say,
"Who will show us any good?"
Yahweh makes the light of His face
Shine upon us.

He fills my heart with greater joy,
Than when the harvest of grain
And new wine abound.
I lie down in peace
And sleep in His shalom ~
The wholeness that comes
From Him alone.
For only Yahweh
Makes me dwell in safety.

Psalm 5 ~ My King

Yahweh is my King and my God.
To Him alone I will pray.
In the morning, He hears my voice.
In the morning, I lay my requests before Him
I wait and I watch
And I look to Him in expectation.

By His great mercy,
I come before Him.
I bow down and worship Him,
As His holy temple,
In whom He dwells.[1]

He leads me in all that is right
And straightens out my path before me.

My heart is light because I trust in Him.
I shout wildly because He defends me.
I jump for joy because I love His name.
For Yahweh blesses those who are right with Him,
He surrounds them with His favor.
He surrounds me with His favor,
All around me, as with a shield.

Psalm 16 ~ The Portion of My Inheritance

I put my trust in Yahweh,
I find my refuge in Him.
He preserves me and protects me.
Everything good in my life
Comes from Him

And I take delight
In all His people.

Yahweh is my portion
And my inheritance.
He is my cup of blessing.
He sustains me and holds my future.
The boundary lines of my life
Have fallen in pleasant places.
Yes, I have a good inheritance.

I will bless Yahweh,
Because He guides me.
I think about Him
In the quiet of the night
And He instructs me
Deep in my heart.

I keep my focus on Him always,
And I will not be fearful of any danger.
So I am lighthearted,
Everything in me
Whirls and twirls
With joy.

For He will not abandon me.
He will show me the path of life.
In His presence is abundant joy
And at His right hand,
Where I am seated with Jesus,[2]
Are pleasures that last forever.

Psalm 18 ~ My Strength in Time of Struggle

I love you, Yahweh, my Strength.
Yahweh my Rock, My Fortress, My Deliverer.
I call upon Yahweh ~
He is worthy of all praise ~
And I am rescued.

When I am in distress,
I call upon Yahweh.
I cry out to my God
And He hears my voice.
My cry comes before Him
And He does not turn
His ear away from me.
He answers and acts
On my behalf.

When I am surrounded by darkness,
Yahweh gives me light.
With Him, I can charge into battle,
By my God, I can leap over barriers.
He is my shield and I trust in Him.

Who is God, except Yahweh?
And who is a rock, except God?
He arms me with strength
And keeps me on the path of victory.
He makes my steps swift and sure,
And sets me in the high places,
Safe and satisfied.

Yahweh trains me for the battle,
With skill and strength.

He shields me with His salvation
And lifts me up by the might of His hand.
His favor makes me increase.
He gives me room to maneuver
Quickly and freely.
By Him, I overcome all my foes.

Yahweh lives!
I bless Him as the Rock of my life,
The God of my salvation.
I give Him thanks
In front of the whole world
And sing praises to His name,
Because He has given me the victory
And has shown me His faithful love.

Psalm 19 ~ The Instruction of Yahweh

The instruction of Yahweh
Is whole and complete;
It makes me come alive.
The testimony of Yahweh is dependable;
When I am foolish,
It makes me wise.
The direction of Yahweh is straight and level,
And fills me with gladness.
The word of Yahweh is clean and clear,
And causes me to see.

Yahweh's honor is pure and lasts forever.
His decisions are always trustworthy and right.
They are richer to me than a fortune in fine gold,
And sweeter than honey fresh from the comb.

They enlighten my way and keep me from danger.
They lead me into a rich, rewarding life.

God instructs me concerning hidden errors
And clears me of faults I did not know.
He pulls me back from willful sins
And will not let them rule over me.
So I am blameless before Him,
Cleansed of a multitude of sins.[3]

I yield the words of my mouth
And the thoughts of my heart
To Yahweh, my Rock and My Redeemer,
And I have favor before His face.

Psalm 20 ~ My Help From Heaven

Yahweh answers me when I am in trouble.
The God of Jacob lifts me out.
He sends me help from His sanctuary,
From the heart of heaven,
From the midst of His people,
From His dwelling place
Deep in my heart.
He remembers the sacrifice,
The blood of Jesus,
Shed on my behalf.[4]

He gives me the desires of my heart
And fulfills my purpose,
The God-given plans He has for me.
I shout for joy because of the victory
He has given me,

And I celebrate the name of our God,
For He has granted all my requests.

Now I know that Yahweh
Takes care of me in every way,
With salvation, prosperity, and victory
From His mighty hand.
Some trust in their own strength,
Their own resources,
But I will remember
And trust in Yahweh our God.
They will collapse and fall
But I will rise up and stand straight.

Psalm 21 ~ Victorious Joy

Yahweh's strength fills me with joy;
I shout wildly because of His salvation ~ Jesus!
He has given me the desires of my heart
And has not held back what I asked of Him.
He brings rich blessings to me
And crowns me with good things.
I asked Him for life
And He gives it to me abundantly,
Forever and ever.

My glory is great in Jesus
What a grand and magnificent life I have in Him!
He has blessed me greatly,
Prosperity without end.
My joy overflows because of His presence.
My confidence is in Yahweh,
So I will not be shaken.

I praise Yahweh for His strength
And sing of the mighty victories
He has won for me.

Psalm 23 ~ My Shepherd

Yahweh is my Shepherd;
I will never be in lack[5],
For He supplies everything I need.
He leads me to abundant, green pastures,
Where I lie down, satisfied.
He refreshes me beside calm waters.
He restores my soul, renews my life.
He leads me in the paths that are right and good
And bring honor to His name.

Even when I walk in the low places
Where death casts its shadow,
I fear no danger,
For my Shepherd is with me.
He will guide me through
And protect me.

Yahweh prepares a table before me,
A rich feast spread for me ~
Right in front of my enemies!
They cannot stop His blessing in my life.

He welcomes me with His favor;
And anoints me with fresh oil
I am revitalized.
He fills my life to overflowing,
With good things.

His faithful love and goodness
Is with me wherever I go,
And I will dwell with Him forever.

Psalm 25 ~ My Whole Life

I lay my whole life before Yahweh.
I trust Him with everything,
He will not let me down.
My expectation is in Him,
He will not leave me hanging.

Yahweh guides me in His ways
And shows me how to live.
He leads me in what is faithful
And teaches me what is true.
He is the God who rescues me,
Prospers me, sets me free.
Everyday I wait and I watch
All the day, for Him.

Yahweh looks at me with compassion,
He thinks of me with His eternal love.
He does not hold my past against me,
But He forgives me out of His tender mercy,
Because He is good.

Yahweh leads me in what is right
And guides me with proper judgment
In the way that is pleasing to Him.
I live in awe of Yahweh and honor Him.
He directs me like an arrow
In the way He wants me to go.

So, I live the good life
And dwell in prosperity,
My children and all my descendants
Shall possess the earth.

Yahweh reveals His secrets to me
And shows me the blessings of His covenant,
I always look to Yahweh
Because He always rescues me,
Sets me free and protects me.
I will live unashamed
Because I trust in Him.

My whole life is before Him
That I may always do what is right,
And He preserves me,
Because I look to Him.

Psalm 26 ~ Yahweh Clears My Name

Yahweh clears my name,
Because my whole life belongs to Him.
He is the one I trust.
He examines me and roots out
Whatever does not belong,
So my heart and my mind
Are pure and blameless before Him.

His covenant love is always in front of me
And I live by His faithfulness and truth.
I come before Him
With a loud voice of thanks,
To declare the wonderful things He has done.

I love the beauty of His habitation
And the glory of His presence.

I will walk in integrity,
The wholeness of who I am in Him
And who He is in me.
He makes me stand on firm and level ground.
I will bless Yahweh with all His people.

Psalm 27 ~ The Goodness of Yahweh in My Life

Yahweh brings light to every part of my life.
He is my salvation, my rescue, my freedom,
My healing, my prosperity, my victory.[6]
Yahweh is the strength of my life.
There is no reason for me to fear anything.

The one thing I really want, I already have.
It is the only thing I need ~
To dwell with Yahweh
All of my life and forever.
I gaze upon His beauty;
It is time well-spent.
I study His ways
And I ask Him about everything.

When trouble comes, He keeps me safe
In the glory of His presence,
Where the enemy cannot see.
He sets me in a place the enemy cannot reach.
Even if I am surrounded,
I still have the advantage,
So I give Yahweh loud shouts of praise.

He speaks to me deep in my heart.
"Seek Me only," He says.
O Yahweh, Your presence is all I want!
He will never turn me away in anger.
He will not leave me or let me go.
Even if everyone else runs away,
Yahweh will still be with me,
The God who rescues me.

Yahweh will direct my way
And lead me in a smooth path,
Even when adversity comes.
My confidence is this:
I will see and enjoy
The goodness of Yahweh in this life.
My expectation is set on Yahweh,
My heart is fixed on Him
And I am encouraged.

Psalm 28 ~ Yahweh's Treasured Ones

I bless Yahweh.
He hears me when I cry out to Him
And answers my prayer.

Yahweh is my strength and my protection.
I trust Him completely,
And He surrounds me with help.
I jump for joy and praise Him
Everywhere I go.

Yahweh is the strength of all His people.
He has anointed us for salvation,

For strength and prosperity,
For health and freedom in Jesus.

He will deliver us and bless us ~
We are His treasured inheritance.
He will guide, protect and provide for us
And carry us like a shepherd,
Now and forever.

Psalm 32 ~ The Happiness of Being Forgiven

O the happiness!
When I crossed the line,
Yahweh forgave me.
When I did wrong,
He pardoned me.
When I came clean,
He did not hold any of it against me

When I was hiding out,
My strength was gone;
I was in anguish.
Conviction was heavy on me
And I was miserable.
But when I admitted I had done wrong,
Yahweh forgave me all
And removed my guilt.[7]

So when I have messed up and done wrong,
I will run quickly to Him,
For He is near, even if I am far away.
And if trouble comes
I will be in the right place,

For He is my safe and secret place.
He will protect me on all sides.
He will see me through,
And I will be shouting for joy.

Yahweh will teach me
And give me direction.
I will keep my eye on Him
And He will guide me.

Those who do wrong
Bring pain and sorrow on themselves,
But those who run to Yahweh
Are surrounded by His faithful love.
My heart is light in Yahweh;
I whirl and twirl and shout for joy
Because of Him.
O the happiness!

Psalm 34 ~ A Brag About Yahweh

I will bless Yahweh at all times,
I will always be singing His praises.
I will brag about Yahweh with every breath,
So the humble may hear and hope
And be light-hearted in Him.
I want everyone to see how great He is
And to praise His name together with me,
With loud and joyful shouts.

I focus diligently on Yahweh
And go to Him about everything.
He hears me and answers my prayer.

He rescues me;
His perfect love casts out my fear.[8]
I look to Him and I am encouraged;
He will not let me down.

When I am in need or afflicted,
I cry out to Yahweh and He hears me;
He rescues me from all my troubles.
Yahweh sends His angels to surround me
He delivers me because I trust in Him
And honor His name.

I have tasted and seen that Yahweh is good.
I turn to Him and ~ O the happiness!
I live in awe of Yahweh and honor Him,
And I have no lack.
I focus on Yahweh and go to Him;
He gives me every good thing.
I enjoy life and experience His goodness everyday,
Because I guard my mouth, my words,
Speaking only what is good and true.

I will not do what is evil,
Only what is good.
I will pursue peace, the shalom,
The wholeness that comes from God alone,
And I will strive to live well with all people.

Yahweh watches over me
And hears me when I cry.
He delivers me out of all my troubles.
When my heart is burdened,
Yahweh is near, to help me.
When I am crushed, He heals me.

Yahweh rescues me because I belong to Him.
I trust in Him, and there is no condemnation.[9]

Psalm 35 ~ Yahweh Contends for Me

Yahweh contends with those who contend with me.
He fights against those who fight against me.
He is the Warrior who stands for me and helps me.
He will stop those who are after me,
Because Jesus is my salvation!
Those who seek my life will be brought to confusion.
But I will whirl and twirl for joy because of Yahweh;
I will delight thoroughly in Jesus, my Champion.

Who is like Yahweh?
He keeps the weak from being overcome
And the poor from being plundered.
He rescues me from destruction
And will not let the enemy triumph over me.
He will clear my name.

Those who stand with me
Will shout for joy and celebrate.
Yahweh will be great in their eyes
Because He takes pleasure
In the prosperity of His people.
I will speak of His faithfulness,
Because He always does what is right,
And I will praise Him continually.

Psalm 36 ~ The Covenant Love of Yahweh

The covenant love[10] of Yahweh fills the heavens.
His faithfulness covers the earth.
All His ways are right and good,
As firm as the mountains.
His judgments are profound,
As deep as the sea.
He sustains every living thing.

The covenant love of Yahweh ~
How incomparable and precious it is to me!
I find my peace in the shadow of His wings.
I feast on the abundance of His house
And drink from the river of His pleasure.
He is the fountain, the source of my life,
And His light causes me to see.
His love for me will never end
And He will lead me in His rightness.

Psalm 37 ~ Possess the Land in Patience

I do not worry when bad people have it good;
I do not envy them; they will not last ~
And their time comes quickly.
I keep my focus on Yahweh;
I trust in Him and keep doing what is good.
I stay put and feed on His faithfulness.

I delight myself in Yahweh,
My heart is pliable before Him.
He brings it into line with His heart.
And gives me all my desires.

For a Life of Faith, Happiness and Awe in God

I commit my way to Yahweh,
I roll it all over onto Him,
Holding back nothing.
I put my confidence in Him,
And He does for me
Whatever needs to be done.
He will bring forth His rightness in me.
He will shine His light on my life
And everyone will see His goodness on me.

So I wait, quietly and patiently,
Before Yahweh.
I do not get agitated
When those who do wrong prosper.
I do not let it get up my nose;
I let go of rage, for it does not help
But only makes things worse.
Those who do wrong will not last,
They will be cut off.
But those who trust in Yahweh
Will possess the land.

So I will wait, quietly and patiently,
Trusting in Yahweh,
And I will possess the land.
I will enjoy the abundance and wholeness
That comes from His shalom, His peace ~
Nothing missing, nothing broken.

Yahweh will take care of me all my days,
And my inheritance will last forever.
He will not let me down in tough times;
Even in famine, I will have more than enough,
To give and to share.

Yahweh directs all my steps,
And they lead me to delight.
Even if I stumble, I will not be down for long;
Yahweh will lift me up again.
Over the years, this is what I have learned:
There is always help for His people,
And bread for their children.
Yahweh loves justice and will set things right;
He will never turn us away.

I think on what is wise and true,
And speak of what is right and good.
Yahweh instructs my heart
And makes my steps sure.
My expectation is in Yahweh;
I walk in His ways.
He will lift me up to possess the land.
His future for me is shalom, peace.
He is my strong place in troubled times;
He will surround me with help
And bring me through.

Psalm 40 ~ Yahweh, My Rescue

I waited with focused expectation before Yahweh.
He bent down and heard my cry.
He lifted me out of the terrible pit I was in.
I was stuck in deep; He pulled me out
And set me on solid ground.

He has given me a new song,
A new opportunity to praise Him.
Now I do my victory dance.

For a Life of Faith, Happiness and Awe in God

Many will see what Yahweh has done;
And be in awe of Him ~
And have hope.

O the happiness of trusting in Yahweh!
I am not dependent upon the arrogant
Or subject to their deceits.
So many marvelous things
Yahweh has done for me.
His thoughts and plans for me
Are wonderful, incomparable.
They are more than I can count.

He has caused me to hear and understand.
My desire is to please Him,
And He instructs my heart.
The good news[11] of Jesus and His rightness
Has done this in me, and I will proclaim it.

Yahweh does not hold back His lovingkindness,
His faithfulness, His tender mercies;
He protects and sustains me.
Yahweh shows favor to His people and rescues them.
He will turn back those who wish me evil
And put to shame those who seek my harm.

But I will be merry and celebrate
And say how great Yahweh is;
He is my rescue and my help
And His thoughts toward me
Are for good.

Psalm 41 ~ The Happiness of Being Helped

O the happiness of helping the poor and the weak!
It is a joy that comes straight from Yahweh's heart.
He will rescue me, too, when I am in trouble;
He will make me smooth in the day of adversity.
Yahweh will protect me on all sides;
I will be happy and prosperous on the earth,
And He will deliver me from the enemy.

Yahweh will give me strength
When I am sick and weak;
He will raise me up and heal me.
He will bend down and show Me His favor;
He will restore my spirit and heal my body.
Yahweh will help me
And the enemy will see his defeat.

Yahweh takes care of me and keeps me going,
Because I belong to Him, fully and completely.
He has set me before His face forever.

O the happiness!

Psalm 46 ~ Abundantly Available Help

God is our shelter and our strength,
Our abundantly available help,
Even in calamity.
So we refuse to be afraid.

When the earth shudders and shakes,
We will not fear.

If the mountains should drop into the sea,
We will not fear.
Though there be earthquakes and tsunamis,
We will not be afraid.

In all these things,
God is still our shelter and our strength
Our abundantly available help.

There is a river that streams from heaven
To the people of God,
His dwelling place on earth,
And makes us glad.
God is with us, His kingdom is in us.
We will not be shaken
Because God will help us
And He will not be late.

Nations rage and kingdoms topple
When God lifts His voice.
But Yahweh, with His angel armies, is with us.
The God who sheltered Jacob
Will be our shelter, too.

This is what we will see,
The wonders of Yahweh,
Bringing war to an end all over the world;
Weapons are useless against Him.
Nations will cease their striving
And will know that He is God
And confess Jesus is King.
He will be praised among the nations
And glorified in all the earth.
Yahweh, with His angel armies, is with us.

The God who lifted Jacob high
Will lift us, also.

Psalm 52 ~ Like a Green Olive Tree

I am like a green olive tree
In the house of God.
The love of God is constant,
And I will trust His faithfulness
Forever and ever.
He will keep His covenant,
The promise He made with me
Through Jesus.[12]

I will give Him praise forever
Because He has done
What He said He would do.
I will keep my focus
And my expectation on God
And proclaim His goodness
Before all His people.

Psalm 56 ~ Yahweh is For Me

When I am being attacked,
Continually harassed by the enemy,
Yahweh shows me His mercy and kindness.
He reveals His favor on my behalf.
Though surrounded by my adversaries,
I will not fear.
I speak the word of Yahweh;
I put His praise on my lips,

His promise in my mouth,
And I trust in Him
With all I've got.

Yahweh keeps track of me,
He knows the tears I have shed;
They are entered into His ledger.
He will turn back the enemy
When I call to Him for help.
This I know, because Yahweh is for me.[13]
I put my trust in Him
And I do not fear what any man can do.

Yahweh fulfills His word
And I declare it to everyone,
With thanks and praise.
He pulls me through
And keeps me from sliding
Over the edge into destruction,
That I may walk with Him
And enjoy life.

Psalm 57 ~ Yahweh in the Storm

When storms rage, I go to Yahweh for refuge.
He will show me His favor and kindness.
He will keep me safe under His wing
While the tempest passes by.

I call out to Yahweh,
Who is much greater than anything
That could ever come my way.
He will do for me

Whatever needs to be done.
He will send whatever I need,
From the realms of heaven,
And rebuke whatever threatens me.
He will display His covenant love
And faithfulness.

Even in the midst of hungry lions
With anger and slander in their mouths,
I will praise Yahweh,
Who reigns over the heavens
And shows His glory over all the earth.
Those who dig a pit for me,
Who set a trap for my steps,
Will fall into it themselves,
While I pass by in safety.

My heart is prepared, focused on Yahweh.
I will sing and celebrate;
I will stir up everything within me
And start every day with praises to Him.
I will give Him thanks
In front of everyone, everywhere.
For His covenant love and faithfulness
Fill heaven and earth.

Psalm 61 ~ When My Heart is Overwhelmed

When my heart is overwhelmed,
When I feel disoriented, dislocated,
Far away from everything dear,
I cry out to God; He listens for me.
He hears and answers my prayer.

He leads me back to solid ground;
He lifts me up and sets me
In a place I could not reach.

God is my shelter, my strong place,
Where I am secure from the enemy.
I will dwell with Him forever,
Safe under His wings.
I have committed myself to God,
To trust Him always.
He hears me.
He has given me the inheritance
Of those who honor His name,
Who live in awe of Him.

He gives me long life ~
I see the generations.
He has set me as a king,
To rule and reign with King Jesus.[14]
I will dwell with Him forever.
His covenant love and faithfulness
Keep watch over me.
I will sing and celebrate His name
And trust Him always.

Psalm 62 ~ God My Calm

Only in God do I find my calm.
My help and my wholeness
Come from Jesus alone.
He is my rock and my strength,
My salvation, my victory, my prosperity,
My fortress and my defense.

Though the enemy seeks to bring me down,
When the dust clears, I will still be standing.
My expectation is set only on Him,
On Jesus alone, my rock and my refuge.
And in Him, I will not be shaken.

God alone is my prosperity and my glory;
Every good thing in my life
Comes from Him.
My rock, my strength, my security
All come from Him.
I will trust in Him at all times.
I will pour out my heart to Him,
Laying every matter before Him,
And He will take care of it all.

God does what no one else can do.
The life of the common man is transient;
The rich and powerful make promises
But cannot deliver.
Only in God do I find my help.

God has spoken this,
And I see it everywhere:
Strength belongs to God,
Faithful love comes from Him,
And He will help all who trust in Him.

Psalm 63 ~ Yahweh is Life and Joy

Yahweh is my God.
I go to Him every morning,
About everything.

All that is in me cries out for Him;
My heart, my mind, my soul, my strength,
Even my body hungers for Him.
Without Yahweh, life is a wasteland.

I look for Yahweh
In His sanctuary,
In His dwelling place
Among His people,
And in my heart.
I contemplate His power and His glory.
His covenant love is better than life;
I would rather die than to live without it.

I will bless Yahweh as long as I live
And lift up my hands in praise to His name.
I am fully satisfied in Him ~ life is a feast!
I sing praises to Him with hoots and hollers.
What joy I have!

I ponder Him as I lay upon my bed,
I think on Him in the middle of the night,
Because He always helps me.
I howl for joy, secure in Him.
I cling to Him with all that is in me,
Because He holds me up
With His powerful hand.

Psalm 66 ~ What Yahweh Has Done for Me

Come and see what Yahweh has done;
Awesome things for His people,
Awesome things for me.

He rules forever,
Revealing His power to every generation.
I will praise Him loudly,
So everyone can hear.
He sustains my life
And gives me a firm footing.

When I was tested,
He was refining me like silver.
I was trapped, burdened, run over.
It was rough.
But He brought me out
To a place of abundance,
A place of freedom and fulfillment.
I give Him thanks and praise,
And bring Him my best.
I belong to Yahweh forever.

All who honor Yahweh,
Come and hear
What He has done for me.
When I was in trouble
I cried out to Him in faith,
With praise in my mouth
And a heart clean before Him.
He heard my cry and helped me.
Praise God!
He hears my prayer
And shows me His faithful love.

Psalm 71 ~ Yahweh All My Days

I put my trust in Yahweh,
He will not let me down.
He sees me through,
Because of His rightness,
Because of His goodness,
Because of His faithfulness.
He hears me and rescues me,
And I am set free.

Yahweh is a secure shelter,
A strong fortress,
Where I can always go for help,
Just as He has promised.
So my expectation is set on Him;
He gets me through the tough times.

I have trusted Yahweh since I was young,
And I am still here to praise Him.
My whole life is a testimony,
Because He is my strong place, my refuge.
So my mouth will be filled with His praise,
To give Him honor and glory everyday.
He will not leave me when I am old
Or abandon me when I am weak.

When the enemy plots against me,
Yahweh is not far from me;
He will come quickly and help me.
The enemy and the accuser
Will be put to shame,
While I add to Yahweh's praise
Day by day.

I will tell again and again
What He has done for me,
Things too many to count.

I will walk in the victory of Yahweh,
Proclaiming His goodness,
Until I have told of His power and strength
To this generation and those yet to come.
He has done great things for me
And there is none like Him.

Though struggles and sorrows come my way,
He revives me when I'm down;
He lifts me up,
Increases my honor,
And gives me His comforts.
I give Him thanks and praise,
And hoop it up with joyful songs,
To tell of His goodness.

Psalm 73 ~ A Sudden Realization

Truly, Yahweh is good to His people,
To those whose hearts belong to Him.
There was a time when I doubted this.
I almost lost my footing
When I saw fools boasting of their success,
And the immoral enjoying prosperity.
Though their ways were wrong,
I envied their results.
They seemed to be thriving,
While I was just surviving.
I was confused.

For a Life of Faith, Happiness and Awe in God

"Has it all been in vain ~
This playing fair and doing what is right?
It doesn't seem to work
And every day feels like a burden."

That is what my mind thought,
But had I opened my mouth
To speak in agreement with it,
I would have been untrue ~
To Yahweh, to His people,
To myself.
My heart knew better,
But when I tried to understand,
It just wore me out.

Then I came into the dwelling place of Yahweh;
I saw the glory of His presence,
And suddenly I realized ~
The wicked and their prosperity do not last!
Their way is precarious
And eventually leads to destruction.
I was foolish to have doubted Yahweh,
I was like an animal
That has no understanding.

The truth is that I am always with Yahweh
And He is always with me,
Holding on to my hand,
Guiding me with His divine wisdom,
And when all is said and done,
He will receive me with glory and honor.

Yahweh in heaven is on my side,
And there is nothing I desire on earth

Apart from Him.
If my body should grow weak
And all my faculties fail,
He will still be the strength of my life
And my inheritance forever.

Those who turn from Yahweh,
Are far away from Him, and will not last.
It is good, then, for me to come close to Yahweh.
I have put my trust in Him;
So shall I tell of all His wonderful works.
Truly, Yahweh is good to His people,
To those whose hearts belong to Him.

Psalm 77 ~ The Tenacity of Faith

I cry out to Yahweh.
I cry out fervently,
Because I know He hears me.
There may be a wait,
But I know He will answer,
And He will not be late.

In my distress I turn to Yahweh.
I pour out my heart
And lift up my hands in prayer.
I will not give up.

I remember Yahweh,
How He helped me in the past.
I bring my complaint to Him;
I ponder and groan,
But I do not give up.

I think of the old days, the good times;
They seem so long ago,
But I do not give up.
I call to mind my songs in the night,
The old songs, the victory songs,
And deep in my heart,
This I know ~

Yahweh has not set me aside.
He is not suddenly displeased with me.
His covenant love has not failed.
His promises are still with me.
He has not forgotten to show His favor.

Though I am overwhelmed,
And it seems like He has changed,
I do not give up,
But I remember again His mighty deeds,
All the wonderful things
Yahweh has done for me.
I will meditate on them,
Ponder them deeply.
For Yahweh does not change,
No matter how I might feel.
God's way is His own business,
And He takes care of His own,
Of those who belong to Him.

Who is as great as Yahweh?
He does wonders
And shows His strength
To His people.
He stretches out His arm
And redeems our lives.

Psalm 81 ~ Fully Satisfied in Yahweh

I hoot and holler
To Yahweh our strength.
I shout out for joy
And bellow a victory song,
Because the God of Jacob
Is my God, too.
It is time for loud music and celebration.

Yahweh ordains festivals,
Merriment for His people.
Because He delivers us
From every oppression,
Removes every burden
From our shoulders,
And we are free.

When I faced adversity,
I cried out to Yahweh.
He stripped away my fears,
Made me strong, and rescued me.
He answered me with thunder
From the chambers of heaven;
He rolled over the enemy
With His lightning.

I listen for Yahweh's voice
And confess His word.
I come into agreement with Him
And follow what He says.
He alone is God
And I will worship no one but Him,
The One who set me free.

I open my mouth wide to Yahweh,
I enlarge my expectation toward Him.
He will satisfy me with abundance
And every good thing.
I love His voice and I walk in His ways.
He subdues my enemy,
Turns His hand against my adversary.
He fills me with the best
And satisfies me with sweetness.

Psalm 84 ~ Yahweh's Dwelling Place

I love the dwelling place of Yahweh,
Lord of the Angel Armies.
How wonderful it is to be in His presence;
It is the delight of my soul.
My whole being cries out for joy
Because of God, who is my life.

O the happiness of dwelling with Yahweh!
I will praise Him everyday, now and forever.
O the happiness of having God as my strength!
My heart is on a journey with Him.
When I pass through the valley of dryness,
It wells up with refreshing springs,
Pools of blessing and prosperity.
The closer I walk with Him,
The stronger I become, day by day,
Until I stand before Him
At journey's end.

Yahweh, Lord of the Angel Armies,
Hears my prayer;

He is attentive to my cry.
Yahweh is my shield, my protector.
He looks upon me with favor
Because of Jesus, His Anointed One.

One day with Yahweh
Is better than a thousand without Him.
Just looking in at His doorway is better
Than dwelling sumptuously with the wicked.

Yahweh is a glorious king,
Our sun and our shield.
Yahweh gives grace and glory;
He does not hold back
Any good thing from me.[15]
O the happiness of trusting in Yahweh,
Lord of the Angel Armies![16]

Psalm 85 ~ The Glory of Yahweh in Our Land

It pleases Yahweh
To show me His kindness,
To set me free and prosper me.
He has forgiven all my wrong
And taken away all my sin.
He turned His anger away from me.
He rescued and restored me.
He revived me and gave me
Reason to rejoice.

Yahweh has shown me His covenant love;
He has given me His salvation ~ Jesus

I will hear what Yahweh says;
It is a word of peace,
Shalom, wholeness,
To His people,
To all who trust and follow Him
Instead of foolishness.

His salvation is very close to me,
Jesus is always with me, in me ~
The divine expectation,
The joyful anticipation
Of glory revealed in me,[17]
That His glory may dwell in our land.

Yahweh's faithful love
Brings forth faithfulness in me.
The rightness of His ways bless me
With peace and prosperity.
It is like heaven on earth.
Yahweh gives what is good
That our land may give its increase.
His way of rightness
Shows us how to live.

Psalm 91 ~ My Sheltering Place

I dwell in the sheltering place of the Most High,
And abide under the shade of the Almighty.
Yahweh is my refuge and my strong place;
He is my God and I trust in Him.

He will surely rescue me
From the trap of the enemy,

And from deadly disease.
He will shelter me, safe beneath His wings.
His faithfulness is my shield and armor.

I will not fear the terror that stalks the night,
The weapon that comes by day,
The sickness that lurks in the darkness,
The destruction that lays waste in plain sight.

A thousand may fall at my side,
Ten thousand at my right hand.
But it shall not come near me.
I will witness, from a safe place,
The result that comes to the wicked.

Yahweh is my refuge,
The Most High is my dwelling place.
No evil will befall me,
No plague will come near my house,
For He gives His angels charge over me,
Orders concerning me,
To protect me in every way.
They take me up with their hands
To keep me from harm.

I walk upon the lion and the cobra;
The strong and cunning deceiver
Is under my feet.

I have set my love upon Yahweh,
And He will deliver me.
He will set me on high,
Because I have known His name.
When I call upon Him,

He will answer me.
He will be with me in trouble,
He will rescue me and set me in a place of honor.
With long life He will satisfy me,
And show me His salvation,
His Yeshua ~ Jesus!

Psalm 92 ~ The Hand of Yahweh in My Life

How good it is to give thanks to Yahweh.
I sing praises and glorify His name:
The Most High ~ there is none greater.
I announce His steadfast love every morning,
I declare His faithfulness every night.
I celebrate them all day long,
Because Yahweh has made me light-hearted
By what He has done for me.

Yahoo! ~ for the hand of Yahweh in my life!
How awesome the things He has done,
How profound His thoughts.
He is able to do exceedingly abundantly
Above all I can ask or imagine,
According to His power at work in me.[18]

Yahweh increases my strength
And continually anoints me
With fresh fire.
I see the defeat of my enemy,
The collapse of those who come against me.

I flourish like a bountiful palm tree
And grow strong and stately like a redwood.

Yahweh has planted me in His house,
And I prosper in His courtyards.
Even when I am old,
I will still bear fruit;
I will remain fresh and green,
Declaring that Yahweh is right
In everything He does.

Psalm 94 ~ Yahweh Sets Things Right

When the enemy comes
To steal, kill and destroy[19],
Yahweh settles the score;
He sets things right
And puts an end to evil.
He pays back the arrogant
What he has earned,
And the wicked
What he deserves.
So I will leave it in Yahweh's hands.

Yahweh teaches me by His Word
And leads me by His Spirit,
And I am very happy because of it.
He instructs me,
Even in the hard times.
He gives me relief from adversity,
Until the wicked are no more.
He will never reject or abandon me,
For I am His own dear treasure.
His judgments set things right,
And those who are right in heart
Will see and follow them.

Yahweh stands up for me
Against those who do evil;
He puts Himself between them and me.
When my foot slips,
Yahweh holds me up,
By His faithful love.
When I am troubled with worry,
Yahweh comforts me,
Calms me down,
Cheers me up.

Yahweh is my strong place,
My safe place,
My solid place.
He will take care of everything for me,
So I will leave it in His hands.

Psalm 101 ~ Honoring Yahweh

I praise Yahweh
Because His love is faithful
And His decisions are wise and just.
I will ponder the way of wisdom ~
Yahweh will help me in this ~
So I may walk with a heart of integrity
Before all who are in my house.

I will set nothing vile before my eyes,
Or entertain such things in my thoughts.
I will have nothing to do
With those who promote them.
Those who are perverse in heart,
I will send away from me;

I will have no regard for them.
I will also have nothing to do
With those who gossip and slander,
Nor will I tolerate arrogance or conceit.

I will show favor to those who are trustworthy
And honor to those who are honorable,
And I will gladly sit with them.
I will walk with those who walk with integrity.

Those who act deceitfully
Will find no place with me,
And I have no time
For those who try to flatter me.
I will be watchful
And I will not associate
With those who embrace evil,
So that I may honor
Yahweh and His people.

Psalm 103 ~ Yahweh's Benefits

Everything in me gives praise to Yahweh.
All my heart, all my soul, all my might
Gives thanks to His name ~
There is none like Him in all the world.
I continually think of His benefits,
All the wonderful things He does for me.
I count on them.

He forgives me ~ of everything!
He heals me of all sickness and disease.
He rescues me from danger and destruction.

For a Life of Faith, Happiness and Awe in God

He crowns me, surrounds me
With His faithful love and tenderness.
He satisfies my desires with good things
And renews my youth like the eagle's.

Yahweh does what is right,
And establishes justice
For all who are oppressed.
He makes His ways known
And shows His mighty works
To His people.

Yahweh is full of grace and mercy;
He is patient with me,
And shows me the abundance
Of His faithful love.
He does not deal with me
According to my sin ~
Jesus took that to the cross
And made me right with God.[20]

As far as heaven is above the earth,
That is how big His love is for me.
As far as the east is from the west,
That is how far He has carried
My sin from me.
As a father is tender toward his children,
That is how Yahweh is toward me.

Yahweh's faithful love for me is forever.
It reaches to my children,
Even my children's children,
Because I am in covenant with Him
And I walk in His ways.

Yahweh has established His throne;
His kingdom rules over all.
I come before Him with boldness
To receive His grace and mercy,[21]
And I am seated at His right hand,
With King Jesus.[22]

Psalm 112 ~ A Life Well-Lived

I live in awe of Yahweh;
I love His instruction
And delight in His ways.
O the happiness!

My descendants will be mighty in the land.
My children, and their children,
And their children's children
Will all be blessed,
Empowered by heaven,
Wealth and riches in our houses.
We walk with Yahweh
And that changes the world,
Now and forever.

We will always have
Light in the darkness.
We will be gracious,
Full of compassion and tenderness.
We will show favor
And lend help to those in need,
And good will come back to us.
We will conduct all our affairs
With sound judgment and integrity.

We will not be shaken by anything;
Yahweh will remember us
And take care of us.
We will not be afraid
When bad news is in the air;
Our hearts are firmly established,
Trusting in Yahweh.
We will not fear the enemy;
We are sustained by the peace of Yahweh.
Nothing will be missing,
Nothing will be broken;
All will be restored, made whole,
And we will rejoice in the victory.

We will give freely to those in need,
For we will always have more than enough
For every good work.
It will show the goodness of Yahweh
And bring praise to His name.[23]
Our influence and honor will increase
And the effect of walking with Yahweh
Will continue to make us a blessing to others.

Psalm 115 ~ All My Glory is in Yahweh

To Yahweh alone
Goes all the glory;
I will praise Him for every good thing in me,
Because of His covenant love
And faithfulness.

I put my confidence in Yahweh;
He is my Helper, my Defender.

He remembers me,
To bless me.
Yahweh blesses all who honor Him,
Who live in awe of Him,
From the greatest to the least ~
And there are no "least" with Him.

Yahweh gives us increase,
Adds more and more to our blessings,
To us and our children.
We are blessed by Yahweh,
Maker of Heaven and Earth.

Heaven belongs to Yahweh,
And He has given the earth
As an inheritance
To all who are His.
His kingdom comes
As His will is done
On earth as in heaven.[24]

We will not be silent
But will praise and adore Yahweh
Now and forever.

Psalm 116 ~ Why I Love Yahweh

I love Yahweh;
Because He hears my voice
And answers the cry
Of my heart.
He turns His ear
And listens closely to me;

For a Life of Faith, Happiness and Awe in God

I will go to Him about everything,
As long as I live.

Yahweh is full of grace and favor,
All He does is right and just.
He is tender and compassionate,
And protects the simple in heart.

When I was down, broken,
He rescued me, lifted me up.
My heart found its peace,
Because Yahweh dealt
Bountifully with me.
He saved my life,
Dried my tears,
Directed my steps
Onto solid ground.
I will walk with Yahweh
And enjoy a life pleasing to Him,
A life of faith.[25]

What thanks shall I give to Yahweh
For all His blessings and benefits?
I will drink deeply
From the cup of salvation,
The cup of healing and deliverance,
The cup of joy in Jesus.
And I will proclaim
The name of Yahweh,
Right here, right now,
In the presence of His people.

The people of Yahweh
Are precious in His sight;

Their death He does not treat lightly
Or allow easily.

O Yahweh, I am Your servant.
I am indeed Your servant,
The son of Your maidservant.[26]

I offer my praise to Yahweh
And declare His name
Right here, right now,
In the presence of His people.

Psalm 118 ~ Giving Thanks to Yahweh

I give thanks to Yahweh,
Because He is good,
Because His covenant love
Is always there for me,
And always will be.

When I was in a tight spot,
I cried out to Yahweh;
He answered me
And set me in a wide place,
An abundant place.

Yahweh is for me,
So I will not be afraid
Of anyone or anything;
They cannot harm me.
The covenant love of Yahweh
Casts out all my fear.[27]

For a Life of Faith, Happiness and Awe in God

Yahweh is for me and He helps me,
So I will look on in victory
Over whatever comes my way.
It is better to trust in Yahweh
Than in the wealth and power of people.

When I was surrounded by the enemy,
I cut them short, subdued them,
By the name of Yahweh.
They surrounded me like stinging bees,
But their fire was quickly put out[28]
By the name of Yahweh.
They pushed me hard to make me fall,
But Yahweh helped me.

Yahweh is the source
Of my strength and my song;
Jesus is most certainly my salvation.
The house of God's people
Rings with loud victory songs
And praises to Jesus.

The right hand of Yahweh
Does mighty things.
The right hand of Yahweh
Is always ready to help me.
Jesus, at the right hand of the Father,
Has done mighty things for me;
He is worthy of all my thanks and praise.

He gives me life,
So I will live and declare
What Yahweh has done for me.
Though trouble came

Yahweh brought me through it,
And He has opened to me the gate
Where His people enter in;
So I will come and give thanks to Yahweh.

I thank Him because He answered me.
I thank Him because Jesus is my victory.
Jesus, the Building Block
Rejected by religious folk,
Has become the Cornerstone
Of God's new building.
Yahweh has done this
And it is marvelous in my eyes.
Yahweh has made this day happen;
I will whirl and twirl for joy
And be light-hearted in it.
I want everyone to know His blessing.

Yahweh sets me in a wide place
An abundant place.
Yahweh gives me prosperity
And causes me to succeed.
I enter in by the name of Yahweh,
Welcomed by His people,
And I am blessed.

Yahweh is God and He gives me light;
I will direct my praise to Him.
He is my God;
I will give Him thanks;
And tell everyone how great He is.

I give thanks to Yahweh,
Because He is good,

Because His covenant love
Is always there for me,
And always will be.
Always.

Psalm 121 ~ I Turn to Yahweh

When I am in distress or need,
Where do I turn for help?
I look to Yahweh;
He is my mountain,
My refuge, my strength.
My help comes from Yahweh,
Maker of Heaven and Earth.

Yahweh will not let me fall
But will set me on firm ground.
He keeps me, guards me,
Sets a hedge all around me.
He is always watching over me
To protect and provide for me.
Nothing sneaks up on Him. Ever.
See, this is how Yahweh is
With all His people,
All who look to Him.

Yahweh is my protector;
He shields me from harm
By day and by night.
Yahweh keeps me from evil and guards my life.
He watches over my comings and goings,
Now and forever.

Psalm 126 ~ Yahweh Frees the Captives

When Yahweh set me free
From the bondage I was in,[29]
It was like living in a dream,
A wonderful dream come true.
My mouth was filled
With shouts of joy and laughter.
It was evident to everyone around
That Yahweh had done
Great things for me.
Indeed, Yahweh has done
Great things for me,
And I am very happy.

But there are many others
Who are still oppressed,
In bondage, held captive;
I cry out to Yahweh
To rescue them and set them free.
Make them like streams
That cause the desert to bloom.
I sow my tears for them,
That I may reap a harvest of joy,
Singing the victory song with them.
I carry this with me,
Sowing the seed wherever I go.
I know I will come again,
Shouting for joy
Because of the harvest.

Psalm 127 ~ A Legacy in Yahweh

We trust in Yahweh
To build our house,
Our family, our legacy.[30]
Otherwise, all our work
Would be pointless.
We trust in Yahweh

To watch over His people,
To hedge us about
With His protection.[31]
Otherwise, all our vigilance
Would be in vain.

It is useless to toil
From morning to night
And go to bed worried.
Yahweh is our source and supply.
He blesses the work of our hands[32]
And gives us His provision,
Even in our rest.

See, children are a heritage,
A divine inheritance,
Yahweh's gift to us.
They are a blessing
And they become our legacy ~
God's gift, and ours,
To the world.

They are like arrows
In the hand of the mighty and skillful,
To be sent forth

With strength and direction.
It is a very happy thing
To have a quiver filled with them.

Yahweh builds our house
And increases it with children;
He builds their houses
And increases them, as well.
They will be mighty in the land
And will prevail at the gates of the city,
With the purpose of God in their hearts
And the wisdom of God in their mouths,
And they shall change the world.

Psalm 128 ~ The Extravagant Blessing

O the happiness
Of following Yahweh,
To love Him, trust Him,
Live in awe of Him
And walk in His ways.

We enjoy the rewards
Of the work of our hands,
The work He has given us.
Yahweh takes care of all our needs.
We are happy and prosperous,
And all is well with us.
We are like a fruitful vine,
Our home like a vineyard,
Our children like olive plants
All around our table.

See, this is how Yahweh wants to bless
All who love Him, trust Him,
And live in awe of Him.[33]
Yahweh blesses us
That we may enjoy
The prosperity of His kingdom
All our days,
And see our children's children
Walk in His blessing
And in His ways.

Psalm 130 ~ Forgiveness and Help

Out of the depths of my soul,
The center of my being,
I cry out to Yahweh;
He hears my voice
And is attentive to my cry for help.
He does not count my sins against me,
Otherwise, I could not stand before Him.
But He forgives me, pardons me, cleanses me,
Because of Jesus,[34]
And I love Him, trust Him,
Live in awe of Him all the more.

I wait patiently for Yahweh;
My expectation is set on Him.
I listen for His voice
And trust in His promise.

I watch for Yahweh,
Intently, diligently,
More than the watchman of the night

Waits for morning.
Yahweh's help will come
As sure as the morning.

Set your expectation on Yahweh,
Trust in His faithful love.
He will rescue you
With the abundance of His help,
And forgive you of everything,
Because of Jesus.

Psalm 131 ~ Quieting Myself in Yahweh

My heart is not lifted up
With pride or self-importance,
As if I have any good thing in me
That did not come from Yahweh.

My eyes are not lifted up in arrogance,
As if I was sufficient of myself
To think anything as of myself.
I have no room for the ego
That eases God out.

I do not concern myself
With things too deep
Or too difficult;
It only gets me agitated,
Frustrated, confused.
And Yahweh does not need my advice.

But I quiet myself, calm myself,
Take my eyes off me and put them on Yahweh.

I am like a young child,
Sitting with its mother,
Trusting that she knows and cares,
That is how my heart is with Yahweh;
He knows and cares.

So I set my expectation on Yahweh
And wait for Him,
Patient and content.
All is well, now and forever.

Psalm 133 ~ Where the Anointing Flows

How good and pleasant it is
For me to walk in unity
With the family of God,
With my brothers and sisters
In King Jesus.

That is where the anointing,
The high priestly anointing,
The anointing of Jesus,
The Anointed One,
Flows freely ~
Faith working through love.[35]

It is like the heavy dew on the mountain,
That refreshes and revives
The people of God.

That is where God promises the blessing,
That is where life comes forth in abundance,
Now and forever.

Psalm 136 ~ Yahweh's Faithful Love for Me

I give thanks to Yahweh
Because He is good,
And His love for me is faithful forever.
I give thanks to Jesus,
Who is King over all kings
And Lord over all lords,
And His love for me is faithful forever.

He is the one who does great wonders,
Because His love for me is faithful forever.
He laid out the heavens and the earth[36]
With skill and understanding,
Because His love for me is faithful forever.

He struck down the enemy,
Destroyed the works of the devil[37]
Because His love for me is faithful forever.
And He brought me out of bondage,
Because His love for me is faithful forever.
He has given me an inheritance,
Heaven on earth,[38]
Because His love for me is faithful forever.
He remembered me with His favor
When I was brought down low,
He lifted me up and rescued me,
Because His love for me is faithful forever.

Yes, I give thanks to Yahweh
Because He is good,
And His love for me is faithful forever.

Psalm 138 ~ Before All the Kings of the Earth

Everything in me
Gives thanks to Yahweh.
I sing His praises
Before all the angels of heaven
Before all the kings of the earth.

I focus on Him in worship,
In the place of adoration,
Among His people
And in my heart.
I praise His name
Because of His covenant love
And faithfulness.

Yahweh has magnified
His Word and His name,
Made them great above everything else.
And He has given to Jesus
The Name that is above all names.[39]

So when I cried out to Yahweh,
He encouraged me, made me bold,
With strength in my soul.

Now all the kings of the earth
Will acknowledge Yahweh
And give Him praise
When they hear His Word.
They will sing about the way of Yahweh
When they see the greatness of His glory.
Because Yahweh, though He is high,
Has regard for the lowly,

But the proud and the arrogant
Do not rate with Him at all.

When I am beat down and in trouble,
Yahweh revives me again;
The power of His right hand
Takes care of all those
Who rage against me.
He does this on my behalf.

Yahweh will bring to completion
Everything He has begun in my life
And fulfill every good purpose
He has prepared for me.
His love for me is faithful forever
And He will never turn me away.

Psalm 139 ~ Yahweh Knows Me

Yahweh has examined me, proved me,
Knows everything about me,
Sees everything in me.
Everything.
He knows my every action
And my every thought,
Even as it is being formed within me.

He winnows all my ways,
Separating the wheat from the chaff.
He is familiar with all my moves.
He is completely aware of every word
That comes out of my mouth,
What I say and what I mean.

Yahweh goes before me
And follows behind me.
He surrounds me on every side,
Above and below.
His hand is always upon me.

His knowledge of me is more wonderful
Than I can comprehend;
He is able to do
Exceedingly abundantly
Above all I can ask or imagine,
According to His power
At work in me.[40]

Everywhere I go,
Yahweh is there already.
Everywhere.
From the highest heights
To the deepest depths;
From the courts of heaven,
Where I am seated with King Jesus,[41]
To the ends of the earth,
He is there with me.
He guides me, protects me,
With His strong hand.

Even if darkness overwhelms me,
It will not hide me from Him.
He sees through it all;
He is Light
And He gives light.

He has made me for Himself,
Formed me in my mother's womb,

Set me apart as His marvelous creation,
His wonderful possession.
Indeed, all His works are marvelous;
I know this deep inside
And I give Him my highest praise.

I am His craftsmanship,
An intricate tapestry,
The handiwork of heaven
And the dust of the earth.
He saw me before I was fashioned,
And designed His purpose for me,
The book of days He desired for me
From the beginning.

How marvelous His thoughts,
How wonderful His plans for me,
They are more than I can number.
Even if I could count them up,
When I added the very last one,
He would still be with me ~
The best of all.

Yahweh examines my heart
And knows my thoughts.
When I go astray,
He restores me to the path
Ancient and eternal ~
Life!

For a Life of Faith, Happiness and Awe in God

Psalm 140 ~ His Victory Over My Enemies

Yahweh rescues me
From those who are evil;
He guards me
From those who do wrong,
Who plot out perversity in their hearts
And stir up strife day after day,
With sharp tongues and poison lips.

Yahweh protects me
From the hand of the troublemaker;
He preserves me from the arrogant,
Who set traps and snares
To trip me up.

Yahweh is my God,
He hears my cry for help.
He is my God, my strength,
My salvation ~ Jesus,
Who brings me out safely.
He covers me in the day of conflict.
The wicked will not get what they want,
Their plans will not succeed,
Their names will not be exalted.
Jesus gives the victory to me,
And His name will be exalted
Above all.

The words of my enemies,
The mischief of their mouths,
Will come back to them,
Upon their own heads.
The snares they have laid

Will cause them to stumble;
The pit they dug for me,
They will fall into themselves.
Their slanders will fail
And they will be overtaken
By people just like them.
This will be of their own doing,
And it will be their undoing.

As for me, my confidence is this:
Yahweh will do justice for the afflicted
And set things right for all those in need.
So I will give Him thanks,
And all who are right with Him
Will be at home in His presence.

Psalm 141 ~ Help in a Time of Evil

I cry out to Yahweh, Come quickly!
He hears me and answers.
I set my prayer before Him like incense,
I lift up my hands to give Him praise.

Set a guard, O Yahweh, over my mouth;
Keep watch over the door of my lips!

Out of the overflow of my heart,
My mouth speaks;
So I will keep my heart with all diligence.[42]
I will not let it be turned toward any evil thing,
Or take part with those who do wrong.
Nor will I honor their ways.

If the righteous reprove me,
It is a kindness to me.
If they correct me,
It is an anointing for my head,
I will receive it and prosper by it,

But my prayer is against the deeds
Of those who do what is evil.
When they are cast aside,
My words will be heard,
Words of healing and hope,
Guided and guarded by Yahweh.

My eyes are on Yahweh, my God.
He will keep me safe
And guide me past
The traps of the enemy,
The snares of the wicked.
They will fall into their own nets,
While I walk safely by.

Psalm 142 ~ When I Feel Abandoned

When I am in distress
I cry out LOUD to Yahweh.
Show me Your favor and kindness!
I pour out my problem to Him,
I lay out my trouble before Him,
I cast my care upon Him,
Because He takes care of me.[43]

When I am overwhelmed,
He knows the path I should take.

He knows the traps that have been laid for me,
And He leads me around them.

When I feel abandoned,
With no one to help,
I cry out to Yahweh;
He is my stronghold,
My shelter, my safety.
He is all I have.
But He is all I need ~
And all I want.

When I am beaten down,
Yahweh hears my cry
And rescues me
From those who attack me,
Those too strong for me.
He brings me out ~
Praise His name!
His people gather around me
(I am never really alone)
For Yahweh is bountiful toward me.

Psalm 143 ~ When My Soul Feels Weak

When the enemy comes after me,
And my soul feels weak,
And my heart is distressed,
I remember days gone by
And all Yahweh has done for me.
I ponder all the ways He works
On my behalf.

For a Life of Faith, Happiness and Awe in God

I stretch out my hands to Him,
Thirsty for Him,
Like a land without rain.
I know He will answer me
And will not let me fade away.
He will not hide His face from me,
He has already revealed it to me
In the face of Jesus the Son.

In the morning
I will hear word of His faithful love
Because I trust in Him.
He will show me
The way I should go,
Because I look to Him.
He will deliver me from my enemies,
Because He is my shelter
And I run to Him.

He will teach me to do
What is pleasing to Him,
Because He is my God.
He will guide me by His Spirit
And lead me on level ground,
Because He is good.

He will revive me,
Because I belong to Him
And bear His name.
He will bring me out of distress
Because He is faithful to His own.
And in His faithful love,
He will cut off all who attack me,
For I am His servant.

Psalm 144 ~ From Battle to Blessing

Blessed is Yahweh, my Rock,
Who has taught me how
To run to the battle
And fight the fight.[44]

He is my faithful one
My fortress, my strong tower,
My rescuer, my shield,
The one in whom I take refuge,
And the one who subdues
Those who come against me.

Who am I, that He should think of me
And show me such favor?
He moves heaven and earth
To give me His aid.
He stretches out His hand
And rescues me out of deep waters.
He delivers me
From those who tell lies,
Who promise peace
But work evil.

I will sing a new song,
A victory song,
And give Him praise.
He rescues us, protects us,
Delivers us from the evil one.

That our sons be
Like mighty oaks,
Full and flourishing.

That our daughters be
Like sculpted pillars,
Strong and beautiful.

That our storehouses
Be filled to overflowing
With all kinds of provision.

That our wealth
And prosperity increase ~
Always having
All sufficiency
In all things,
And abundance
For every good work.[45]

That there be
Nothing missing,
Nothing broken,
Nothing lost or stolen.

This is what He has planned
For all His people.
We are happy and blessed indeed.

Psalm 145 ~ My King and My God

I exalt Jesus,
My King and my God,
With the highest honor.
Every day I bless His name,
I will brag on Him
Now and forever.

He is great beyond all things,
More than I can tell,
And worthy of all praise.

This generation
Will announce His works
To the coming generations,
Proclaiming His mighty acts,
And I will celebrate His glory,
His splendor, His majesty.

We will tell of His awesome power
That sets things right,
And I will give testimony
To His greatness.

We will pour out songs of praise
Because His goodness knows no end.
We will shout and howl for joy
Because everything He does
Is faithful and true.

He is full of favor and compassion,
And exceedingly patient with us;
His love is constant.
His goodness is for everyone,
He surrounds everything
With kindness and mercy.

Everything He has made
Will give Him thanks,
And all who are His
Will kneel in adoration.

For a Life of Faith, Happiness and Awe in God

The glory of His kingdom
Will be our testimony,
The power of His dominion
The word we bring.
His dominion is forever,
He is King over all generations.

He sustains those
Who have no strength,
Lifts up those
Who are pressed down.
He has provision
For everyone and everything,
And opens His hand
To satisfy every need.

He is near to those
Who call on Him,
To all who trust Him.
He shows favor to those
Who honor Him,
And satisfies their desires.
He hears their prayers
And rescues them,
Heals them, prospers them.
He protects those
Who love Him.

My mouth will praise King Jesus,
With all God's creatures,
Now and always.

Psalm 146 ~ All My Life is All About Him

Praise Yah![46]
Everything in me
Praises Yahweh.
All my life,
As long as I live,
Is all about Him.

I do not trust in presidents,
Or senators, or governors,
Or any other human being.
Their help is too small,
Not near enough
For what I need.
They may have good intentions,
But they are unreliable.
And when they die,
Their plans die with them.

But, O the happiness!
Of trusting in Yahweh,
Of setting my expectation
On Him.

The God who helped Jacob
Is the God who helps me.
The God who made heaven and earth
Is faithful and true forever.

He sets things right
For those who are oppressed.
He provides for those
Who are in need.

For a Life of Faith, Happiness and Awe in God

Yahweh frees the prisoner.
Yahweh makes blind eyes see.
Yahweh lifts up those beaten down ~
Stands them up straight.
Yahweh loves those who do right.
Yahweh protects the outsider.
He is a father to the fatherless
And a husband to the widow.
But those who do evil,
He brings to nothing.

Yahweh is King forever;
Jesus rules over all generations.

End Notes

1. In the New Testament, we learn that those who believe in King Jesus the Messiah have become, both individually and all together, the temple — the dwelling place — of God. "Do you not know that you are the temple of God and that the Spirit of God dwells in you?" (1 Corinthians 3:16). "Coming to Him [Jesus] as to a living stone, rejected indeed by men, but chosen by God and precious, you also, as living stones, are being built up a spiritual house, a holy priesthood, to offer up spiritual sacrifices acceptable to God through Jesus Christ" (1 Peter 2:4-5).
2. "But God, who is rich in mercy, because of His great love with which He loved us, even when we were dead in trespasses, made us alive together with Christ (by grace you have been saved), and raised us up together, and made us sit together in the heavenly places in Christ Jesus, that in the ages to come He might show the exceeding riches of His grace in His kindness toward us in Christ Jesus. For by grace you have been saved through faith, and that not of yourselves; it is the gift of God." (Ephesians 2:4-8)
3. "If we walk in the light as He is in the light, we have fellowship with one another, and the blood of Jesus Christ His Son cleanses us from all sin ... If we confess our sins, He is faithful and just to forgive us our sins and to cleanse us from all unrighteousness." (1 John 1:7,9)
4. "But you have come ... to Jesus the Mediator of the new covenant, and to the blood of sprinkling that speaks better things than that of Abel." (Hebrews 12:24)
5. "And God is able to make all grace abound toward you, that you, always having all sufficiency in all things, may have an abundance for every good work" (2 Corinthians 9:8).
6. The Hebrew word for "salvation" in this psalm is *yesha* and can have all of these meanings: deliverance, rescue, liberty, safety, welfare, victory, prosperity, and healing. Which one do you need in your life today?
7. 1 John 1:7,9
8. "There is no fear in love; but perfect love casts out fear" (1 John 4:18).
9. "There is therefore now no condemnation to those who are in Christ Jesus" (Romans 8:1).
10. The Hebrew word translated as "love" in many English versions is *hesed*. It is the love God has covenanted to always show to His people and do good to them. Various translations render it as mercy, faithful love, steadfast love and lovingkindness. *Yahweh* is the name by which God reveals Himself in covenant relationship with His people.
11. The Hebrew text here (Psalm 40:6-9) uses gospel language. The Septuagint, an ancient Greek translation of the Hebrew Scriptures, here uses the word *euangelizo*, to evangelize, to proclaim the good news. See Hebrews 10:5-10, where the author applies this passage to Jesus.

12 "But now He [Jesus] has obtained a more excellent ministry, inasmuch as He is also Mediator of a better covenant, which was established on better promises" (Hebrews 8:6).

13 "What then shall we say to these things? If God is for us, who can be against us? He who did not spare His own Son, but delivered Him up for us all, how shall He not with Him also freely give us all things? Who shall bring a charge against God's elect? It is God who justifies. Who is he who condemns? It is Christ who died, and furthermore is also risen, who is even at the right hand of God, who also makes intercession for us. Who shall separate us from the love of Christ?" (Romans 8:31-35).

14 God has seated King Jesus at His right hand in the heavenlies, "far above all principality and power and might and dominion" (Ephesians 1:20-21). And He has made *us* alive and raised *us* up and seated *us* together in the heavenlies with King Jesus, in the place of ruling and reigning (Ephesians 2:4-6). This is not just future hope, it is present reality for all who are in Jesus.

15 "He who did not spare His own Son, but delivered Him up for us all, how shall He not with Him also freely give us all things?" (Romans 8:32).

16 Speaking of God's angels, the author of Hebrews says, "Are they not all ministering spirits sent forth to minister for those who will inherit salvation?" (Hebrews 1:14).

17 "To them God willed to make known what are the riches of the glory of this mystery among the Gentiles: which is Christ in you, the hope of glory" (Colossians 1:27).

18 "Now to Him who is able to do exceedingly abundantly above all that we ask or think, according to the power that works in us, to Him be glory in the church by Christ Jesus to all generations, forever and ever. Amen" (Ephesians 3:20-21).

19 Jesus said, "The thief does not come except to steal, and to kill, and to destroy. I have come that they may have life, and that they may have it more abundantly" (John 10:10).

20 "For He [God] made Him [Jesus] who knew no sin to be sin for us, that we might become the righteousness of God in Him" (2 Corinthians 5:21). "For the death that He died, He died to sin once for all; but the life that He lives, He lives to God. Likewise you also, reckon yourselves to be dead indeed to sin, but alive to God in Christ Jesus our Lord" (Romans 6:10-11). "There is therefore now no condemnation to those who are in Christ Jesus" (Romans 8:1).

21 "Let us therefore come boldly to the throne of grace, that we may obtain mercy and find grace to help in time of need" (Hebrews 4:16).

22 God has "made us alive together with Christ ... and raised us up together, and made us sit together in the heavenly places in Christ Jesus" (Ephesians 2:5-6).

23 "God is able to make all grace abound toward you, that you, always having all sufficiency in all things, may have an abundance for every good work ... For the administration of this service not only supplies the needs of the saints, but also is abounding through many thanksgivings to God, while, through the proof of this ministry, they glorify God for the obedience of your confession to the gospel of Christ, and for your liberal sharing with them and all men, and by their prayer for you, who long for you because of the exceeding grace of God in you" (2 Corinthians 9:8, 12-14).

24 Adapted from the prayer Jesus taught us to pray (Matthew 6:10).

25 But without faith it is impossible to please Him, for he who comes to God must believe that He is, and that He is a rewarder of those who diligently seek Him" (Hebrews 11:6).

26 This is very personal for me as I think of my mother and my grandmother, both mighty women of God who have now gone to be with Jesus.

27 "There is no fear in love; but perfect love casts out fear" (1 John 4:18).

28 "Above all, taking the shield of faith with which you will be able to quench all the fiery darts of the wicked one" (Ephesians 6:16).

29 Jesus fulfills what was written by the prophet Isaiah, "The Spirit of the LORD is upon Me, because He has anointed Me to preach the gospel to the poor; He has sent Me to heal the brokenhearted, to proclaim liberty to the captives and recovery of sight to the blind, to set at liberty those who are oppressed; to proclaim the acceptable year of the Lord" (Luke 4:18-21). Peter proclaimed that "God anointed Jesus of Nazareth with the Holy Spirit and with power, who went about doing good and healing all who were oppressed by the devil, for God was with Him" (Acts 10:38).

30 "Blessed shall be the fruit of your body, the produce of your ground and the increase of your herds, the increase of your cattle and the offspring of your flocks ... And the LORD will grant you plenty of goods, in the fruit of your body, in the increase of your livestock, and in the produce of your ground" (Deuteronomy 28:4, 11).

31 "The LORD will cause your enemies who rise against you to be defeated before your face; they shall come out against you one way and flee before you seven ways" (Deuteronomy 28:7).

32 "The LORD will command the blessing on you in your storehouses and in all to which you set your hand, and He will bless you in the land which the LORD your God is giving you ... The LORD will open to you His good treasure, the heavens, to give the rain to your land in its season, and to bless all the work of your hand" (Deuteronomy 28:8, 12).

33 See Deuteronomy 28:1-14.

34 "If we confess our sins, He is faithful and just to forgive us our sins and to cleanse us from all unrighteousness" (1 John 1:9). "There is therefore now no condemnation to those who are in Christ Jesus" (Romans 8:1).

35 "For in Christ Jesus neither circumcision nor uncircumcision avails anything, but faith working through love" (Galatians 5:6).

36 "All things were made through Him [Jesus], and without Him nothing was made that was made" (John 1:3).

37 "For this purpose the Son of God was manifested, that He might destroy the works of the devil" (1 John 3:8). "Inasmuch then as the children have partaken of flesh and blood, He Himself likewise shared in the same, that through death He might destroy him who had the power of death, that is, the devil, and release those who through fear of death were all their lifetime subject to bondage" (Hebrews 2:14-15).

38 "Do not fear, little flock, for it is your Father's good pleasure to give you the kingdom" (Luke 12:32). The kingdom of God is wherever the will of God is done on earth as in heaven. See The Kingdom of Heaven on Earth: Keys to the Kingdom of God in the Gospel of Matthew.

39 "Therefore God also has highly exalted Him and given Him the name which is above every name, that at the name of Jesus every knee should bow, of those in heaven, and of those on earth, and of those under the earth, and that every tongue should confess that Jesus Christ is Lord, to the glory of God the Father" (Philippians 2:9-11).

40 Ephesians 3:20

41 Ephesians 2:4-6

42 "A good man out of the good treasure of his heart brings forth good; and an evil man out of the evil treasure of his heart brings forth evil. For out of the abundance of the heart his mouth speaks" (Luke 6:45). "Keep your heart with all diligence, for out of it spring the issues of life" (Proverbs 4:23).

43 "Therefore humble yourselves under the mighty hand of God, that He may exalt you in due time, casting all your care upon Him, for He cares for you" (1 Peter 5:6-7).

44 "For though we walk in the flesh, we do not war according to the flesh. For the weapons of our warfare are not carnal but mighty in God for pulling down strongholds, casting down arguments and every high thing that exalts itself against the knowledge of God, bringing every thought into captivity to the obedience of Christ" (2 Corinthians 10:3-5). "Finally, my brethren, be strong in the Lord and in the power of His might. Put on the whole armor of God, that you may be able to stand against the wiles of the devil. For we do not wrestle against flesh and blood, but against principalities, against powers, against the rulers of the darkness of this age, against spiritual hosts of wickedness in the heavenly places. Therefore take up the whole armor of God, that you may be able to withstand in the evil day, and having done all, to stand" (Ephesians 6:10-13).

45 2 Corinthians 9:8

46 The Hebrew word for "praise" is *hallel*; *Yah* is a shortened form for Yahweh. When we say *Hallelujah*, we are saying *Praise Yah!*

ALSO BY JEFF DOLES

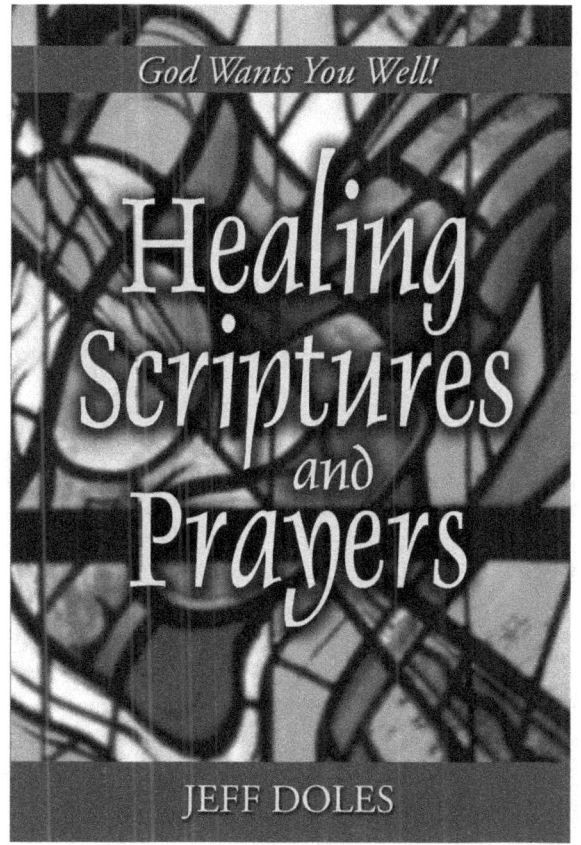

Healing Scriptures and Prayers

ISBN 978-0-9744748-1-6
6 x 9 in. 120 pages

Available at www.walkingbarefoot.com

ALSO BY JEFF DOLES

Praying With Fire
Change Your World with the
Powerful Prayers of the Apostles

ISBN 978-0-9744748-6-1
6x9 in., 104 pages

Available at www.walkingbarefoot.com

ALSO BY JEFF DOLES

There is Always Joy!
Bite-Sized Studies Through the Book of Philippians

ISBN 978-0-9823536-4-6
5.5 x 8.5 in., 125 pages

Available at www.walkingbarefoot.com

ALSO BY JEFF DOLES

The Focus of Our Faith
Bite-Sized Studies Through
the Book of Colossians

ISBN 978-0-9823536-3-9
5.5 x 8.5 in., 151 pages

Available at www.walkingbarefoot.com

ALSO BY JEFF DOLES

Keeping the Faith When Things Get Tough
Bite-Sized Studies Through the Book of First Peter

ISBN 978-0-9823536-2-2
5.5 x 8.5 in., 93 pages

Available at www.walkingbarefoot.com

ALSO BY JEFF DOLES

Miracles and Manifestations of the Holy Spirit in the History of the Church

ISBN 978-0-9744748-9-2
9.6x7.4 in., 274 pages

Available at www.walkingbarefoot.com

ALSO BY JEFF DOLES

The Kingdom of Heaven on Earth
Keys to the Kingdom of God
in the Gospel of Matthew

ISBN 978-0-9823536-0-8
6x9 in., 194 pages

Available at www.walkingbarefoot.com

ALSO BY JEFF DOLES

God's Word in *Your* Mouth
Changing Your World Through Faith

ISBN 978-0-9744748-8-5
6x9 in., 140 pages

Available at www.walkingbarefoot.com

ALSO BY JEFF DOLES

Walking Barefoot
Living in Prayer, Faith and the Power of God

ISBN 978-09744748-0-9
6x9 in., 140 pages

Available at www.walkingbarefoot.com

ALSO BY JEFF DOLES

Let Earth Receive Her King
Advent, Christmas and the Kingdom of God

ISBN 978-0-9823536-5-3
5.5 x 8.5 in., 94 pages

Available at www.walkingbarefoot.com

ALSO BY JEFF DOLES

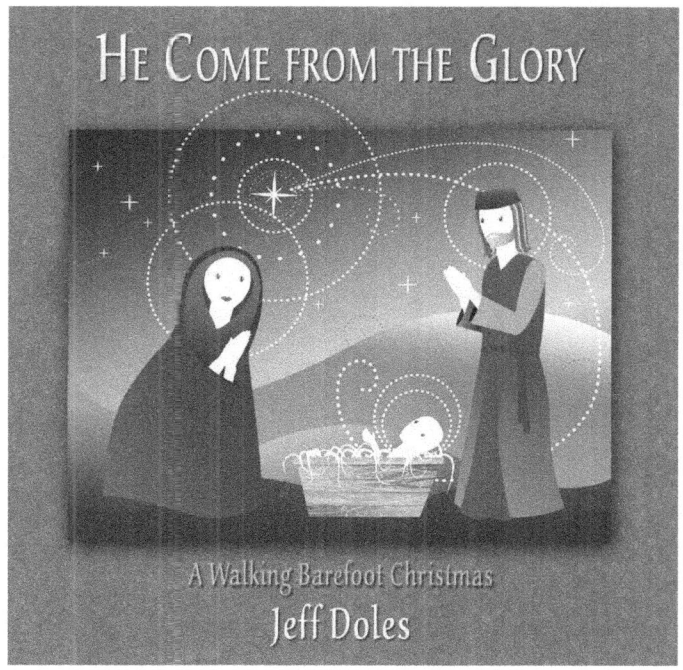

On This Pilgrim's Way
A Walking Barefoot Hymnal

Available in CD and MP3
Listen to audio clips and order at
www.walkingbarefoot.com

www.ingramcontent.com/pod-product-compliance
Lightning Source LLC
Chambersburg PA
CBHW031453040426
42444CB00007B/1076